Essential Question
What can animals in stories teach us?

THE Spider AND THE Honey Tree

by Ann Weil

illustrated by Ethan Long

Chapter 1

A Lazy Spider

There was a clever girl who lived in a village and had a remarkable skill. She could always find the best things to eat. It was her secret.

A spider lived there, too. Spider loved to eat, but he was too lazy to go out and find food himself. "Please take me with you when you go looking for things to eat," Spider begged the girl.

"I've never done that before," she said. "Do you promise to keep my secrets?"

"You can trust me," said Spider.

"What do you like to eat best?" the girl asked politely. "Tell me and I will help you find it."

"I'm fond of plums, and bananas are nice," said Spider. "But most of all, I love honey!"

The girl began to lead Spider into the bush. Spider was thrilled because his plan was working. He had tricked the girl into sharing her secrets.

Chapter 2

Finding Secret Fruits

The girl stopped at a tree. There were only a few ripe plums hanging from its branches, and most people would have walked right by it.

"This tree has the sweetest plums," the girl said. "They are juicy and delicious!"

Spider was greedy as well as lazy, so he pushed past the girl and began to snatch the fruit off the tree. He ate every single plum! He did not leave any for the girl, and he did not even say "Thank you." How rude!

Spider's belly was full, but he was greedy and wanted to feast on more fruit. *This girl is a fool,* he thought, *so I will trick her again.* "Do you know where to find some bananas?" he asked with a smile. "I am very fond of bananas."

"Of course," she said. "Follow me."

Spider could not believe his luck. It was so easy to get all the food he wanted! He raced down out of the tall tree before the girl could change her mind.

"Over here is a small patch of the very best bananas," said the girl. Again, Spider pushed past the girl. He climbed the banana plants and ate all the ripe bananas. Again, he left nothing for the girl, and again, he did not say "Thank you!"

His belly was as full as it had ever been, but Spider was greedy and wanted more. "Have you eaten enough, or would you like to come with me to find some honey?" the girl asked politely.

Spider loved honey most of all. Once more, he waddled out of the tree and followed the girl before she had a chance to change her mind.

Chapter 3

The Honey Tree

The girl led Spider deeper and deeper into the bush until, finally, she stopped at a tree. "This is a very special tree," she said, pointing at a small hole just above her head. "Inside there you will find the most delicious honey you ever tasted."

Spider raced up the tree and squeezed into the hole. Spider was very pleased with himself. He had tricked the girl into giving away her secrets.

In fact, the girl was much smarter than Spider, and she had not fallen for his sneaky plan. She had her own plan to teach this greedy spider a lesson. She remembered that Spider loved honey, and she had saved this place for last on purpose.

Chapter 4

Spider Gets Stuck!

Spider ate all of the sweet golden honey. The greedy creature did not leave even one drop for the girl, and again, he didn't even say "Thank you." Then, when he was all done, he started to climb out of the tree, but he couldn't get out of the hole. His fat, full stomach was much too big.

"Oh no! Help me!" he cried. "I am trapped!"

"It serves you right. You wouldn't be stuck if you hadn't been so selfish," said the girl.

"I'm sorry! Please help me," cried Spider.

The girl laughed. "I am not as foolish as you think. You aren't sorry for what you did. You are only sorry you got stuck."

Spider had never thought his idea would turn into such a problem for him. "Please call for help!" he begged.

The girl smiled. "Help! Help!" she said in a soft whisper. "A rude spider is stuck inside the honey tree. Help! Somebody come and help this greedy spider!" Of course, no one heard her whispered cries.

"Goodbye, Spider," said the girl. She began to walk away. "I am going to get some huge oranges for my family, and you can eat some too, of course. If you want some oranges, just follow me."

Stories like this fable teach lessons, or morals. The moral of this fable is: "Don't be greedy!"

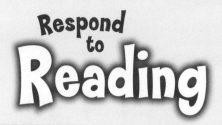

Respond to Reading

Summarize

Use important details to summarize *The Spider and the Honey Tree*.

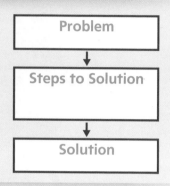

Problem

↓

Steps to Solution

↓

Solution

Text Evidence

1. How do you know *The Spider and the Honey Tree* is a fable? Identify the story elements. **GENRE**

2. What is Spider's problem at the beginning of the story? Reread to identify the problem. **PROBLEM AND SOLUTION**

3. Use your knowledge of suffixes to help you figure out the meaning of *politely* on page 9. **SUFFIXES**

4. Write about why the girl helped Spider find food. **WRITE ABOUT READING**

Compare Texts

Read another fable about a girl and a spider.

 The Girl and the Spider

Changchang knew where to find sweet fruit and honey. Spider followed her.

"You look so hungry!" Changchang said to him. "Come with me to my secret apricot tree and I'll share the fruit with you."

But Spider ate all the ripe apricots by himself. His stomach grew huge, but Changchang did not seem to notice. "You still look hungry. I'll take you to my secret peach tree."

17

When they got there, Spider gobbled up every peach. His belly looked about to burst, but Changchang just said, "Ready for dessert?"

The greedy spider nodded and tried to run after her, but his giant stomach slowed him down. "Wait!" he cried, losing sight of the girl.

"Over here," called Changchang. She was standing beside her boat.

"Are we leaving?" Spider was disappointed. "I was hoping for some honey for dessert."

"Here it is," said Changchang as she pointed to some tree branches hanging over the river.

Spider waddled up the tree, found the honey inside the tree trunk, and slurped down every last drop. With nothing left to eat, Spider waddled back toward Changchang, who was smiling brightly. "That girl is a fool," he said to himself. Just then, a gust of wind blew the big, fat Spider into the water.

"Help!" he cried. "The fish will eat me!" But Changchang was already paddling home.

The moral of this story is: "Greed can lead to losing everything."

Make Connections

What lesson can you learn from *The Girl and the Spider*? ESSENTIAL QUESTION

Compare these two animal stories. How do they teach us something? TEXT TO TEXT

Focus on
Literary Elements

Dialogue Dialogue is what the characters in a story say.

What to Look For As you read a story, look for quotation marks. They show where dialogue begins and ends. Look at this example from the story:

"This tree has the sweetest plums," the girl said.

Your Turn

Write a short animal story with dialogue. Make sure you use quotation marks around the words each character says.

Find a partner and take turns reading your stories aloud. Try reading the dialogue in different voices. Work together and read your stories to the class.